Published by Creative Education
P.O. Box 227, Mankato, Minnesota 56002
Creative Education is an imprint of The Creative Company
www.thecreativecompany.us

Design and Production by The Design Lab
Printed in the United States of America

Photographs by Corbis (Tom Bean, Gary Braasch, Michael & Patricia Fogden. Werner Forman,
Historical Picture Archive, Wolfgang Kaehler, Charles & Josette Lenars, Craig Lovell, Franklin
McMahon, Galen Rowell, John Van Hasselt, Brian A. Vikander), Dreamstime (Quintanilla),
Getty Images (Taxi), iStockphoto (Edward Davis), North Wind Picture Archives (18)

Library of Congress Cataloging-in-Publication Data
Riggs, Kate.
Machu Picchu / by Kate Riggs.
p. cm. — (Places of old)
Includes index.
ISBN 978-1-58341-709-6
1. Machu Picchu Site (Peru)—Juvenile literature.
2. Incas—History—Juvenile literature.
3. Incas—Antiquities—Juvenile literature.
4. Peru—Antiquities—Juvenile literature. I. Title. II. Series.
F3429.1.M3R54 2008   985'.37—dc22   2007051893

First edition

2 4 6 8 9 7 5 3 1

MACHU PICCHU

by Kate Riggs

CREATIVE EDUCATION

MACHU PICCHU (*MAH-choo PEE-choo*) is an old city. It is in the South American country of Peru. It was a sacred city to

4

the people who lived there long ago. They built it as a special place to honor their gods.

Machu Picchu was built high in the Andes mountains

People called the Inca (*ING-kuh*) built Machu Picchu. The Incas were farmers. But they were also great builders. They had a large empire.

The Incas worshiped the god of the sun. His name was Inti.

Many statues (left) were found in Machu Picchu (above)

The Incas built Machu Picchu in the shape of the letter "U." They hauled large white stones called granite up the mountainsides. Then they cut the stone apart into blocks. They used lots of stone to build the city!

This round temple was an important building

Children sell food in towns close to Machu Picchu

The potato was an important **crop** *to the Incas. They grew more than 200 kinds of potatoes!*

The Inca and many other peoples worshiped the sun

Machu Picchu was an important city. The people who ruled the empire lived there. They worshiped their gods in buildings called temples there. Some people watched the sky from the tops of the temples. They kept track of how the sun and the moon moved across the sky.

Inca rulers were often pictured in stone carvings

Rainforests are all around Machu Picchu. A long time ago, the forest grew over the city. It was hidden for a long time. Now, only ruins of the city are left.

12

The huge stone calendar was placed up high

Some of the best stonework can be seen in temples

Inca people kept track of the days by using a calendar made out of stone.

Hiram Bingham called Machu Picchu "The Lost City"

A man from America named Hiram (*HI-rum*) Bingham found Machu Picchu in 1911. He helped people imagine what it had looked like hundreds of years ago.

The round Temple of the Sun at Machu Picchu was the most important building in the city.

The Inca used small tools to chip away at stones

About 300,000 people visit Machu Picchu each year. There are more people there today than when the Incas lived there! Tour guides take visitors on hikes up the mountain.

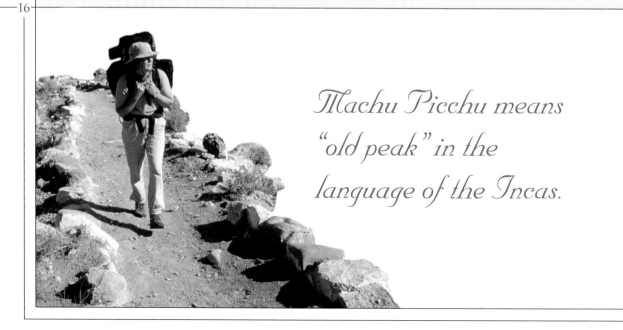

Machu Picchu means "old peak" in the language of the Incas.

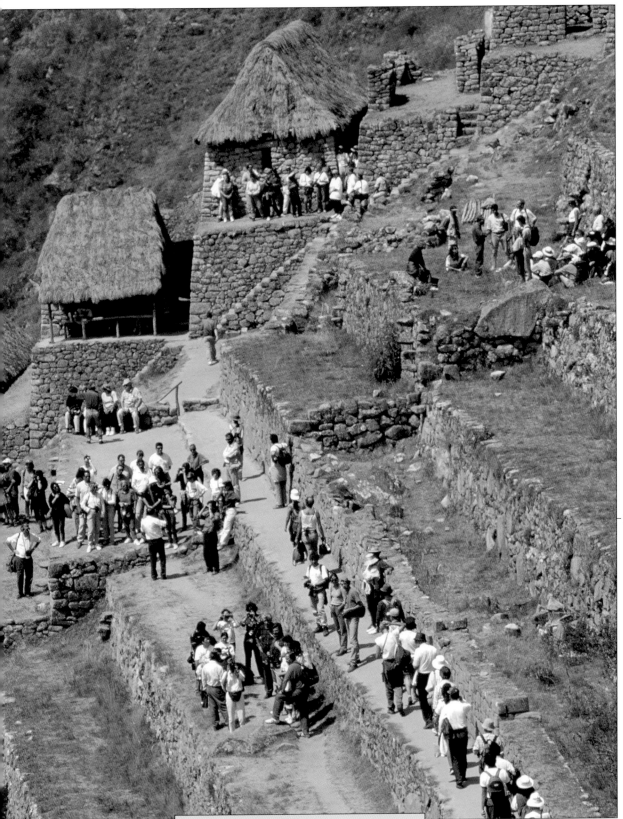

Visitors hike up dirt paths to see the city

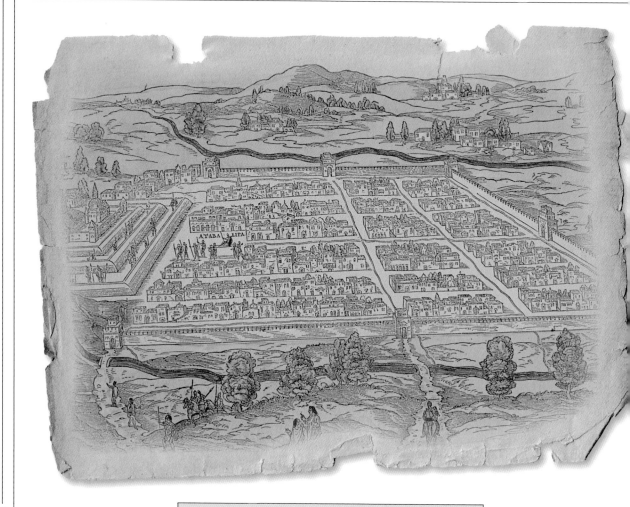

Cusco was at the center of a very large empire

Another Inca city called Cusco (KOOZ-koh) was the **capital** *of the empire. People still live in Cusco.*

Lots of people visit Machu Picchu between May and September. It is warm and dry in Peru then. Many people like to see the animals that live close to Machu Picchu. Llamas, parrots, and lizards all live on the mountain.

Peru is home to about 53 kinds of parrots

Machu Picchu is the biggest tourist site in Peru

When people visit Machu Picchu,
they can see how important it was to

the Incas' culture. Today, it is a special place for the whole world to enjoy.

Llamas can be seen eating on the hillsides nearby

glossary

capital
the most important city in a country, state, or empire

crop
a plant that is grown for food

culture
all the things that make up the way that people live

empire
a large area of land (and any people living there)
controlled by one ruler

ruins
what is left of a building after no one has taken care of it
for a long time

sacred
something that is holy and set apart for a special reason

read more about it

Braman, Arlette. *The Inca: Activities and Crafts from a Mysterious Land*. Hoboken, N.J.: Jossey-Bass, 2003.

Lewin, Ted. *Lost City: The Discovery of Machu Picchu*. New York: Philomel/Penguin, 2003.

index